Archer Press
P.O. Box 2790
Turlock, CA 95380
www.archerpress.com

Thanks

First off I'd like to thank you for purchasing my book. I've very excited about it and hope that you are able to use the information to get some money to make it easier to afford your college degree. I'm always open to feedback and would love to hear from you. If you get a scholarship, have one to add to the next edition of the book or anything else drop by and see me at thecollegescholarshipblog.com. Also, be on the lookout for our upcoming scholarship books, "1001 College Scholarships" and "76 Scholarships for the Military and Their Families."

Ten Tips for Successful Scholarship Applications:

1. **Ensure You Are Eligible** - Don't waste time applying for scholarships that you are not eligible for. While the vast majority of the scholarships listed here are open to anyone, most scholarships have specific requirements before applying. If you don't meet those requirements don't waste your time, you won't win.

2. **Do Your Best** – While you may want to apply to every scholarship that you can find, you probably won't have enough time to get quality applications in to all of them. Narrow your search down to what you can handle. Then do your best to apply, with high quality

and error free applications and supporting documents.

3. **Follow the Instructions** – It may sound crazy, but many, many applications come in with missing documents or sections not filled out. Double check to make sure you are following the instructions and have completed all the sections.

4. **Keep it Clean** – Cleanliness does count. Keep the pizza and soda stains off your application and make sure that you can read everything.

5. **Watch the Calendar** – Each and every scholarship has a deadline. When reviewing your scholarships write down the deadlines on a calendar. Also, don't forget to get your submission turned in before the deadline. Some won't accept it after that date, regardless of the post mark date.

6. **Be Yourself** – Many scholarships require an essay. It is important to be yourself. One scholarship listed in this book limits the applications they'll accept to 10,000. That is a lot of applications. Rather than trying to just give them what you think they want, give them who you are.

7. **Proofread** – Proofread your essay….and then, proofread again.

8. **Get References** – You'll probably need letters of recommendation. Don't just get the easiest, go for the best. See if your principal,

counselor or someone else who knows you and can speak to your qualifications in regard to the scholarship requirements.

9. **Keep Your Money** – Don't ever pay money to apply for a scholarship. Don't listen to guarantees or promises. As my grandmother always said, if it sounds too good to be true, it probably is. Don't pay an application fee, ever.

10. **Proofread** – Did I say this one already? Proofread your application.

The Scholarships

(1) $1,000 "A GPA Isn't Everything" Montly Scholarship

URL:http://www.cappex.com/page/account/quickApply.jsp?scholarshipID=gp&code=HO1002-5-
Goal: To help deserving students pay for college.
Eligibility: Applicants must be in high school or college or plan to attend college in the next 12 months.
Target: Applicants must be in high school, college or non-traditional students.
Amount: $1,000
Number: 12
Based on Financial Need: No
Deadline: Last day of each month.
Apply online only

---

(2) $1,000 MoolahSPOT
MoolahSpot
2713 Newlands Avenue
Belmont, CA 94002

URL:http://www.moolahspot.com/index.cfm?scholarship=1

Goal: The $1,000 MoolahSPOT Scholarship is sponsored by MoolahSPOT.com and helps students of any age pay for higher education. The scholarship is a competition based on a short essay. Family income, grades and test scores are not used in selecting a winner. The award must be used for any education-related expenses such as tuition, fees, books and room and board.

Eligibility: Any student at least 16 years or older who plans to attend, or is currently attending, college or graduate school. Students may be of any nationality and reside in any country. Students may study any major or plan to enter any career field at any accredited college or graduate school. Although applicants can be from any country, all applications must be completed in English.

Target: Any high school, undergraduate or graduate student.

Amount: $1,000

Number: Varies

Based on Financial Need: No

Deadline: April, August, December

Apply online only

---

(3) $,1500 College JumpStart Scholarship

College JumpStart Scholarship Fund
4516 B10 El Camino Real No. 325
Los Altos, CA 94022

URL:http://www.jumpstart-scholarship.net

Goal: To help students who are committed to using education to better your life and that of your family and/or community.

Eligibility: Applicants must be in 10th, 11th or 12th grade in high school or college. Scholarship open to non-traditional students. Applicants may study any major and attend any school in the US and must be legal residents of the US. The scholarship can be used for tuition, room and board, books and other educational expenses.
Target: High school students, College students and Non-traditional students.
Amount: $1,500
Number: 3
Based on Financial Need: No
Deadline: April and October
Apply online only

---

(4) $1,500 Scholarship Detective Launch Scholarship

Scholarship Detective
URL:http://www.scholarshipdetective.com/scholarship/index.cfm
Goal: To help students pay for college.
Eligibility: Applicants must be in high school, college or a non-traditional student and a US Citizen or permanent resident. The scholarship can be used at any college for any major.
Target: Applicant must be in high school, college or a non-traditional student.
Amount: $1,500
Number: 3
Based on Financial Need: No
Deadline: May, August, December
Apply online only

(5) $2,000 "No Essay" College Scholarship
URL:https://collegeprowler.com/scholarship/apply.as px?source=sc
Goal: To help students pay for college related expenses.
Eligibility: Applicants must be in college or planning to enroll in the next 12 months. The winner is chosen by random drawing.
Target: High school, undergraduate, graduate or non-traditional students.
Amount: $2,000
Number: 12
Based on Financial Need: No
Deadline: Last day of each month at 11pm EST. Apply online only.

---

(6) Americorps National Civilian Community Corps
AmeriCorps
1201 New York Ave NW
Washington, DC 20525
Phone: 202-606-5000
Fax: 202-606-3472
Email: questions@americorps.org
URL:http://www.americorps.gov
Goal: To strengthen communities and develop leaders through national and community service.
Eligibility: Applicants must be U.S. citizens between the ages of 18 and 24. Recipients must live on a AmeriCorps campus in Denver, Sacramento, Perry Point, Maryland or Vicksburg, Mississippi. Applicants must commit to 10 months of service projects that are within the region of the campus.

Target: High school, college, graduate and adult students.
Amount: $5,550
Number: Varies
Based on Financial Need: No
Deadline: Varies
Applications are available online.

---

(7) Americorps Vista
AmeriCorps
1201 New York Ave NW
Washington, DC 20525
Phone: 202-606-5000
Fax: 202-606-3472
Email: questions@americorps.org
URL:http://www.americorps.gov
Goal: To provide financial assistance in exchange for community service.
Eligibility: Applicants must be U.S. citizens who are at least 17 years old. They must be able to serve in a one year, full time position at a nonprofit organization or a local government agency fighting illiteracy, helping communities or health services.
Target: High school, college, graduate and adult students.
Amount: Up to $5,550
Number: Varies
Based on Financial Need: No
Deadline: Varies
Applications are available online.

---

(8) AXA Achievement Community Scholarship

AXA Achievement Scholarship
c/o Scholarship America
One Scholarship Way
St. Peter, MN 56082
Phone: 800-537-4180
Email: axachievement@scholarshipamerica.org
URL: http://www.axa-equitable.com/axa-foundation/community-scholarships.html
Goal: To assist outstanding high school seniors.
Eligibility: Applicants must be U.S. citizens or legal residents and be high school seniors in the U.S. or Puerto Rico. They must be planning on attending a two year or four year accredited college or university in the fall following their high school graduation. They must be ambitious and driven, determined to set and reach goals and respectful of self, family and the community and able to succeed in college. The award is based on the strength of the applicant.
Target: High school students.
Amount: $2,000
Number: Varies
Based on Financial Need: No
Deadline: February
Applications are available online. A completed application, transcript, personal essay and one letter of recommendation are required.

---

(9) AXA Achievement Scholarships
AXA Achievement Scholarship
c/o Scholarship America
One Scholarship Way
St. Peter, MN 56082
Phone: 800-537-4180
Email: axachievement@scholarshipamerica.org

URL: http://www.axa-equitable.com/axa-foundation/AXA-achievement-scholarship.html
Goal: To assist ambitious students with educational expenses.
Eligibility: Applicants must be U.S. citizens or legal residents and be high school seniors in the U.S. or Puerto Rico. They must be planning on attending a two year or four year accredited college or university in the fall following their high school graduation.Applicants must be U.S. citizens or legal residents and be high school seniors in the U.S. or Puerto Rico. They must be planning on attending a two year or four year accredited college or university in the fall following their high school graduation. They must be ambitious and driven, determined to set and reach goals and respectful of self, family and the community and able to succeed in college. The award is based on the strength of the applicant. Only the first 10,000 applications will be accepted.
Target: High school students.
Amount: $10,000-$25,000
Number: 52
Based on Financial Need: No
Deadline: December
Applications are available online. A recommendation form from an adult who can attest to the student's achievement is required.

---

(10) Best Buy @ 15 Scholarship Program
Best Buy Children's Foundation
7601 Penn Avenue S.
Richfield, MN 55423
Phone: 612-292-6397
Email: bestbuy@scholarshipamerica.org

URL:http://www.bestbuy-communityrelations.com/scholarship.htm
Goal: To assist high school students (grades 9-12) that will be attending a college, university or vocational school following high school.
Eligibility: Applicants must be currently in 9th to 12th grade living in the U.S. or Puerto Rico with a minimum GPA of 2.5, with demonstrated commitment and involvement to community service. The award is based on academic performance and community service or work experience. School leadership can also be a consideration. Best Buy employees and/or relatives who qualify are eligible for the scholarship.
Target: High school students.
Amount: $1,000
Number: Up to 1,200
Based on Financial Need: No
Deadline: February
Applications are available online.

---

(11) Best Buy Scholarships
Best Buy Children's Foundation
7601 Penn Avenue S.
Richfield, MN 55423
Phone: 612-292-6397
Email: bestbuy@scholarshipamerica.org
URL:http://www.bestbuy-communityrelations.com/scholarship.htm
Goal: To assist students in affording college.

Eligibility: Applicants must be in high school and living in the U.S. or Puerto Rico. The students must live within 75 miles of a Best Buy store and have a minimum GPA of 2.5 and have work or community experience. They must plan to enter college as a full time student at a two year or four year college the fall after high school graduation.
Target: High school students.
Amount: $1,000
Number: Up to 1,200
Based on Financial Need: No
Deadline: February
Applications are available online. A completed application and transcripts are required when applying.

---

(12) Burger King Scholars Program
Burger King Scholars Program
5505 Blue Lagoon Drive
Miami, FL 33126
Phone: 507-931-1682
Email: burgerkingscholars@scholarshipamerica.org
URL:http://www.bkmclamorefoundation.org/Home
Goal: To assist high school seniors who have part-time jobs with educational expenses.

Eligibility: Applicants must be high school students in the U.S., Canada, and Puerto Rico and must be U.S. or Canadian residents. Applicants must have at least a 2.5 GPA and work part time (averaging 15 hours a week unless there are extenuating circumstances), participate in community service activities, show a financial need, and plan to enroll in an accredited two or four year college, university or vocational/tech school in the fall or summer following their graduation from high school.
Target: High school students.
Amount: $1,000 to $50,000
Number: Varies
Based on Financial Need: Yes
Deadline: January
Applications are available online.

---

(13) Carson Scholars
Carson Scholars Fund
305 W. Chesapeake Avenue
Suite L-020
Towson, MD 21204
Phone: 887-773-7236
Email: caitlin@carsonscholars.org
URL:http://www.carsonscholars.org
Goal: To assist students who show academic excellence and community service.

Eligibility: Applicants must be nominated by their school. They must have a GPA of 3.75 or higher in English, reading, language arts, math, science, social studies and foreign language and be in grades 4 - 11. Applicants must attend a four year college or university after graduation and must have completed community service beyond what is required by their school.

Target: Junior high and younger, High school students.

Amount: $1,000

Number: Varies

Based on Financial Need: No

Deadline: January

Applications are available from the schools of those who are nominated. Only one student can be nominated per school.

---

(14) C.I.P. Scholarship

College is Power
1025 Alameda de las Pulgas No. 215
Belmont, CA 94002
URL:http://www.collegeispower.com/scholarship.cfm

Goal: To assist college students aged 18 and over with educational expenses.

Eligibility: Applicants must be 18 an over and attending or planning to attend a two- or four-year college or university in the next 12 months. Applicants must be U.S. citizens or permanent residents. Scholarship funds can be used for full or part time study in person or online.

Target: High school, College and Adult students.

Amount: $1,500

Number: Varies
Based on Financial Need: No
Deadline: May, August, December
Applications are available online.

---

(15) Charles Shafae' Scholarship
Papercheck
Phone: 866-693-3348
Email: scholarships@papercheck.com
URL:http://www.papercheck.com
Goal: To assist students who have written the best essay.
Eligibility: Applicants must be legal residents of the U.S. or must have a valid student visa, as well as be enrolled, full-time, as an undergraduate student at an accredited four year college or university. Applicants must have a 3.2 GPA or higher, be in good academic standing, and write an essay on a topic selected by Papercheck.
Target: College and Adult students.
Amount: $500
Number: 2
Based on Financial Need: No
Deadline: May
Applications are available online. A completed application and essay are required.

---

(16) Church Hill Classics "Frame My Future" Scholarship
Church Hill Classics
594 Pepper Street
Monroe, CT 06468
Phone: 800-477-9005

Fax: 203-268-2468
Email: info@diplomaframe.com
URL:http://www.framemyfuture.com
Goal: To assist students with their educational expenses.
Eligibility: Applicants must be high school seniors or eligible for graduation in the school year of the application or currently attending college. Applicants must be U.S. residents. A photography, essay, painting or other creative entry is required and the work needs to communicate "This is How I Frame My Future." Employees of Church Hill Classics and all affiliated companies, their families and individuals from the same households are not eligible.
Target: High school, College and Adult students.
Amount: $1,000
Number: 5
Based on Financial Need: No
Deadline: March
Applications are available online. An entry form and piece of original art is required to apply.

---

(17) CKSF Scholarships
Common Knowledge Scholarship Foundation
P.O. Box 290361
Davie, FL 33329
Phone: 954-262-8553
Email: info@cksf.org
URL:http://cksf.org
Goal: To assist high school and college students.
Eligibility: Applicants must register with CKSF online and complete quizzes on various topics. Students must be U.S. high school students in grades 9-12 or in college.

Target: High school, College, Graduate and Adult students.
Amount: $250-$2,500
Number: Varies
Based on Financial Need: No
Deadline: Monthly
Applications are available online.

---

(18) Coca-Cola All-State Community College Academic Team
Coca-Cola Scholars Foundation
P.O. Box 442
Atlanta, GA 30301
Phone: 800-306-2653
Email: questions@coca-colascholars.org
URL:http://www.coca-colascholarsfoundation.com
Goal: To assist community college students with educational expenses.
Eligibility: Applicants must be currently enrolled at a community college and have a GPA of 3.5 or higher and be on track to earn an associates degree or bachelors degree. One student from each state will win a $2,000 scholarship, Fifty students will win a $1,500 scholarship, fifty students will win a $1,250 scholarship and fifty students will win a $1,000 scholarship.
Target: College and Adult students.
Amount: $1,000 to $2,000
Number: 200
Based on Financial Need: No
Deadline: December
Applications are available online. Applicants must be nominated by the schools nominator.

(19) Coca-Cola Scholars Program

Coca-Cola Scholars Foundation
P.O. Box 442
Atlanta, GA 30301
Phone: 800-306-2653
Email: questions@coca-colascholars.org
URL:http://www.coca-colascholarsfoundation.com
Goal: The mission of the Coca-Cola Scholars Foundation is to provide scholarship programs and alumni enrichment opportunities in support of exceptional peoples' thirst for knowledge and their desire to make a difference in the world.
Eligibility: Applicants must be high school seniors in the U.S. who will attend an accredited U.S. college or university. The award is based on character, personal merit and commitment.
Target: High school students.
Amount: $10,000 - $20,000
Number: 250
Scholarship can be renewed.
Based on Financial Need: No
Deadline: October
Applications are available online.

(20) College Answer $1,000 Scholarship

College Answer
Sallie Mae
300 Continental Drive
Newark, DE 19714
URL:http://www.collegeanswer.com

Goal: To assist students with their educational expenses.

Eligibility: Applicants must be high school, undergraduate or graduate students and register on the CollegeAnswer website. A registered user is randomly selected in a monthly drawing.

Target: High school, College, Graduate and Adult students

Amount: $1,000

Number: 1 per month.

Based on Financial Need: No

Deadline: Monthly

To enter the scholarship register online.

---

(21) College Prep Scholarship for High School Juniors

QuestBridge
120 Hawthrone Avenue Suite 103
Palo Alto, CA 94301
Phone: 888-275-2054
Fax: 650-653-2516
Email: questions@questbridge.org
URL:http://www.questbridge.org

Goal: To assist low income high school juniors with admission to leading colleges.

Eligibility: Applicants must be high school juniors with an annual household income of less than $60,000.

Target: High school students.

Amount: Varies

Number: Varies

Based on Financial Need: Yes

Deadline: March

Applications are available online starting in February. A completed application, transcripts and one letter of recommendation is required to apply.

(22) CollegeNET Scholarship
CollegeNET Scholarship Review Committee
805 SW Broadway Suite 1600
Portland, OR 97205
Phone: 503-973-5200
Fax: 503-973-5252
Email: scholarship@collegenet.com
URL: http://www.collegenet.com
Goal: To assist college students and future college students.
Eligibility: Applicants must sign up at the website and participate in their forums. The winner is chosen by user votes on their website.
Target: High school, College and Adult students.
Amount: $3,000-$5,000
Number: Varies
Based on Financial Need: No
Deadline: Weekly
Applications are available online.

(23) Congressional Black Caucus Spouses Education Scholarship
Congressional Black Caucus Foundation
1720 Massachusetts Avenue NW
Washington, DC 20036
Phone: 202-263-2800
Fax: 202-775-0773
Email: info@cbcfinc.org
URL:http://www.cbcfinc.org

Goal: To assist students pursuing an undergraduate and graduate degree.

Eligibility: Applicants do not need to be African American, but must reside or attend school in a congressional district that is represented by a CBC member. Students must attend or plan to attend college full time and must have a 2.5 GPA or above and demonstrate leadership qualities.

Target: High school, College, Graduate and Adult students.

Amount: Varies

Number: Varies

Based on Financial Need: No

Deadline: Varies

Applications are available online.

---

(24) Create Real Impact Contest

Impact Teen Drivers
Attn: Create Real Impact Contest
P.O. Box 161209
Sacramento,CA 95816
Phone: 916-733-7432
Email: info@impactteendrivers.org
URL:http://www.createrealimpact.com

Goal: To increase awareness of the danger of distracted driving.

Eligibility: Applicants must be legal U.S. residents between 15 and 22 years old. They must be enrolled full time at a secondary or post-secondary school. Each applicant must submit an original video, music, creative writing or artwork. Award selection is based on project concept, message, effectiveness and creativity. Projects must be on the topic of distracted driving, entries on drunk driving will not be accepted.

Target: High school, College and Graduate students.
Amount: $500
Number: Up to 20
Based on Financial Need: No
Deadline: June
Entry instructions are available online.

---

(25) CrossLites Scholarship Contest

CrossLites
1000 Hold Avenue
1178
Winter Park, FL 32789
Phone: 407-833-3886
Fax:
Email: crosslites@gmail.com
URL:http://www.crosslites.com
Goal: The CrossLites Scholarship Award was created to provide high school, undergraduate, and graduate students with a chance to learn about Dr. Charles Parker, become inspired, and win some money.
Eligibility: Applicants must be high school, undergraduate or graduate students. Students must write an essay that is between 400 and 600 words based on one of Dr. Charles Parker's quotes or messages that are listed on the website. Each school level (high school, undergraduate and graduate) have their own awards. The award is given based on the judges score (10%) and votes from website visitors (90%).
Target: High school, College, Graduate and Adult students.
Amount: Up to $2,000
Number: 33
Based on Financial Need: No

Deadline: December
Applications are available online. An essay, transcripts and basic contact information is required to apply.

---

(26) Delete Cyberbullying Scholarship Award
Delete Cyberbulling
2261 Market Street #291
San Francisco, CA 94114
Email: applications@deletecyberbullying.org
URL:http://www.deletecyberbullying.org
Goal: To encourage students to commit to deleting cyberbullying.
Eligibility: Applicants must be U.S. Citizens or permanent residents who are attending or planning to attend an accredited college or university in the U.S. for undergraduate or graduate study.
Target: High school, College, Graduate and Adult students.
Amount: $1,500
Number: 2
Based on Financial Need: No
Deadline: June
Applications are available online. A completed application and essay are required to apply.

---

(27) Dell Scholars Program
Michael and Susan Dell Foundation
P.O. Box 163867
Austin, TX 78716
Phone: 512-329-0799
Fax: 512-347-1744

Email: apply@dellscholars.org
URL:http://www.dellsccholars.org
Goal: To assist underprivileged high school seniors.
Eligibility: Applicants must be in an approved college readiness program and they must have a 2.4 GPA or higher. Applicants must be starting a bachelors degree in the fall immediately after their high school graduation. Students must be U.S. citizens or permanent residents and demonstrate financial need. The award is based on "individual determination to succeed," future goals, hardships that have been overcome, self motivation and financial need.
Target: High school students.
Amount: Varies
Number: Varies
Scholarship can be renewed.
Based on Financial Need: Yes
Deadline: January
Applications are available online.

---

(28) Direction.com College Scholarship
Direction
10402 Harwin Drive
Houston, TX 77036
Phone: 713-773-3636 x1500
Fax: 281-754-4959
Email: customer_service@direction.us
URL:http://www.direction.com
Goal: To assist U.S. college students.

Eligibility: Applicants must be high school seniors or current college students. Students must submit an essay on the topic provided that is related to computers. Essay submissions are judge 50% on academic merit and 50% on creativity. Photos are recommended, but not required.
Target: High school, College and Adult students.
Amount: $300 to $1,000
Number: 6
Based on Financial Need: No
Deadline: May
No application is required. Applicants are to send their contact information and completed essay to information@direction.com.

---

(29) Discus Awards College Scholarships
Discus Awards
7101 Wisconsin Avenue Suite 750
Bethesda, MD 20814
Phone:
Fax:
Email: info@discusawards.com
URL:http://www.discusawards.com
Goal: To assist college bound high school students.
Eligibility: Applicants must be U.S. high school students who are involved or have achievements in at least three of the following areas: academics, art, athletics, community service, faith, government, green technology, work or other achievements. The award selection is based on merit.
Target: High school students.
Amount: $2,000
Number: 10
Based on Financial Need: No
Deadline: Monthly

Applications are available online. A completed application and supporting documents are required to apply.

---

(30) Doodle 4 Google
Google
1600 Amphitheatre Parkway
Mountain View, CA 94043
Phone: 650-253-0000
Fax: 650-253-0001
Email: doodle4google-team@google.com
URL:http://www.google.com/doodle4google
Goal: To develop creativity in United States school students by way of a logo contest.
Eligibility: Applicants must be elementary or secondary school students in the 50 U.S. states or Washington D.C. who have registered for the contest.
Target: Junior high or younger, High school students.
Amount: Up to $15,000
Number: Varies
Based on Financial Need: No
Deadline: March
Applications are available from schools that are participating.

---

(31) Dr. Arnita Young Boswell Scholarship
National Hook-Up of Black Women Inc.
1809 East 71st Street
Suite 205
Chicago, IL 60649
Phone: 773-667-7061

Fax: 773-667-7064
Email: nhbwdir@aol.com
URL:http://www.nhbwinc.com
Goal: To acknowledge adult students for their academic achievement.
Eligibility: Applicants must be undergraduate or graduate students. Award selection is based on academic accomplishments in addition to involvement in school and community activities along with an essay.
Target: College, Graduate and Adult students.
Amount: $1,000
Number: Varies
Scholarship can be renewed.
Based on Financial Need: No
Deadline: March
Applications are available by mail.

---

(32) Dr. Wynetta A. Frazier Sister to Sister Scholarship

National Hook-Up of Black Women Inc.
1809 East 71st Street
Suite 205
Chicago, IL 60649
Phone: 773-667-7061
Fax: 773-667-7064
Email: nhbwdir@aol.com
URL:http://www.nhbwinc.com
Goal: To assist women who are going back to school without support of family or spouse.
Eligibility: Applicants must have taken a break in their education because of employment, caring for children or because of a financial issue.
Target: Graduate and Adult students.

Amount: $500
Number: 2
Based on Financial Need: No
Deadline: Varies
Applications are available by mail.

---

(33) Educational Advancement Foundation Merit Scholarship
Alpha Kappa Educational Advancement Foundation Inc.
5656 S. Stony Island Avenue
Chicago, IL 60637
Phone: 800-653-6528
Fax: 773-947-0277
Email: akaeaf@akaef.net
URL:http://www.akaeaf.org
Goal: To assist students for community service and involvement.
Eligibility: Applicants must be full time college students in their sophomore year or higher with a 3.0 GPA or higher. They must have demonstrated community service.
Target: College, Graduate and Adult students.
Amount: Varies
Number: Varies
Based on Financial Need: No
Deadline: April for Undergraduates and August for Graduate students.
Applications are available online. A completed application, personal statement and three letters of recommendation are required to apply.

---

(34) Educational Advancement Foundation Financial Needs Scholarship

Alpha Kappa Educational Advancement Foundation Inc.
5656 S. Stony Island Avenue
Chicago, IL 60637
Phone: 800-653-6528
Fax: 773-947-0277
Email: akaeaf@akaef.net
URL:http://www.akaeaf.org
Goal: To assist students with a financial need.
Eligibility: Applicants must be full time college students in their sophomore year or higher with a 2.5 GPA or higher. They must have demonstrated community service and a financial need.
Target: College, Graduate and Adult students.
Amount: Varies
Number: Varies
Based on Financial Need: Yes
Deadline: April for Undergraduates and August for Graduate students.

Applications are available online. A completed application, personal statement and three letters of recommendation are required to apply.

---

(35) Executive Women International Scholarship Program

Executive Women International
3860 South 2300 East
Suite 211
Salt Lake City, UT 84109
Phone: 801-355-2800
Fax: 801-355-2852
Email: ewi@ewiconect.com

URL:http://www.executivewomen.org
Goal: To assist high school students with their educational goals.
Eligibility: Applicants must be high school juniors who are planning to pursue a four year degree at an accredited college or university.
Target: High school students.
Amount: $1,000-$5,000
Number: Varies
Based on Financial Need: No
Deadline: April
Applications are available by request from the local chapter of the Executive Women International.

---

(36) Families of Freedom Scholarship Fund

Family Travel Forum
891 Amsterdam Avenue
New York,NY 10025
Phone: 212-665-6124
Fax: 212-665-6136
Email: editorial@travelbigo.com
URL:http://www.travelbigo.com
Goal: To award college bound students who have written the best essay.
Eligibility: Applicants must be members of the Travelbigo.com online community and be between 13 and 18 years old. They must be in grades 8 to 12 and attending a U.S. or Canadian high school or junior high school (homeschools are included). They must submit an original essay about a significant travel experience that occurred in the last three years and that happened when the applicant was 12 to 18 years old. The award is based on the essay's originality, quality of storytelling and grammar.

Target: Junior high and High school students.
Amount: $200 to $1,000
Number: 3
Based on Financial Need: No
Deadline: August
Application information is available online. A completed submission form and essay are required to apply.

---

(37) Foundation for Global Scholars General Scholarship
Foundation for Global Scholars
12050 North Pecos Street
Suite 320
Westminster, CO 80234
Phone: 303-502-7256
Email: kbrockwell@foundationforglobalscholars.org
URL:http://www.foundationforglobalscholars.org
Goal: To assist college students from North America study abroad.
Eligibility: Applicants must be U.S. or Canadian students who area at a North American college or university. Applicants must be enrolled in a degree program that will allow for international study and transfer credits to be applied towards the degree.
Target: College and Adult students.
Amount: $500 to $1,500
Number: Varies
Based on Financial Need: No
Deadline: Varies
Applications are available online. A completed application, transcripts and essay are required to apply.

(38) From Failure to Promise Essay Contest
From Failure to Promise
P.O. Box 352
Olympia Fields, IL 60461
Phone: 708-252-4380
Fax:
Email: drcmoorer@gmail.com
URL:http://www.fromfailuretopromise.com
Goal: To assist college students.
Eligibility: Applicants must be high school seniors, undergraduate or graduate students who are planning to enroll or enrolled in a U.S. college or university. A GPA of 3.0 or higher is required and applicants must submit an essay about how the book, "From Failure to Promise: An Uncommon Path to Professoriate" has impacted their pursuit of success. The award is based on the essay's originality, presentation and the quality of the research.
Target: High school, College, Graduate and Adult students.
Amount: $500 to $1,500
Number: 3
Based on Financial Need: No
Deadline: July
Applications are available online. A completed application, transcripts and essay are required.

---

(39) GE-Reagan Foundation Scholarship Program
Ronald Reagan Presidential Foundation
40 Presidential Drive Suite 200
Simi Valley, CA 93065

Phone: 507-931-1682
Fax:
Email: ge-reagan@scholarshipamerica.org
URL:http://www.scholarshipamerica.org/ge-reagan
Goal: To acknowledge students who show leadership, drive, integrity and citizenship.
Eligibility: Applicants must be high school seniors and be planning to pursue a bachelor's degree in the fall following their high school graduation.
Applicants must have a 3.0 GPA or higher, show financial need, and be a U.S. citizen.
Target: High school students.
Amount: $10,000
Number: Up to 20
Scholarship can be renewed.
Based on Financial Need: Yes
Deadline: January
Applications are available online. Applications will not be accepted once 25,000 applications are accepted.

---

(40) Gen and Kelly Tanabe Student Scholarship
2713 Newlands Avenue
Belmont, CA 94002
Phone: 650-618-2221
Fax:
Email: tanabe@gmail.com
URL:http://www.genkellyscholarship.com
Goal: To assist high school, college and graduate students with their educational expenses.
Eligibility: Applicants must be high school, college or graduate students who are legal U.S. residents. Students can attend any college and study any major.

Target: High school, College, Graduate and Adult students.
Amount: $1,000
Number: Varies
Based on Financial Need: No
Deadline: July and December
Applications are available online.

---

(41) Holocaust Remembrance Project Essay Contest
Holland and Knight Charitable Foundation
P.O. Box 2877
Tampa, FL 33601
Phone: 866-HK-CARES
Fax:
Email: holocaust@hklaw.com
URL:http://holocaust.hklaw.com
Goal: To acknowledge high school students who have written an essay about the Holocaust.
Eligibility: Applicants must be 19 years old or younger and currently enrolled in grades 9 to 12. Applicants must submit an essay about the Holocaust and the scholarships entry form.
Target: High school students.
Amount: Up to $5,000
Number: Varies
Based on Financial Need: No
Deadline: April
Applications and essays are submitted online.

(42) Horatio Alger Association Scholarship Program

Horatio Alger Association
Attn: Scholarship Department
99 Canel Center Plaza
Alexandria, VA 22314
Phone: 703-684-9444
Fax: 703-684-9445
Email: association@horatioalger.com
URL:http://www.horatioalger.com
Goal: To assist students who are pursuing a bachelors degree who have demonstrated financial need, academic achievement, community service and integrity.
Eligibility: Applicants must be entering college by the fall after their graduation from high school. They must also demonstrate financial need ($50,000 or less per family) and be involved in community and extracurricular activities. A GPA of 2.0 or higher is required.
Target: High school students.
Amount: $20,000
Number: 104
Based on Financial Need: Yes
Deadline: October
Applications are available online.

---

(43) Joseph S. Rumbaugh Historical Oration Contest

National Society of the Sons of the American Revolution
1000 S. Fourth Street
Louisville, KY 40203
Phone: 502-589-1776

Email: contests@sar.org
URL: http://www.sar.org
Goal: To encourage students to learn about the Revolutionary War and its impact on America.
Eligibility: Applicants must prepare a five to six minute speech on an aspect of the Revolutionary War. The contest is open to high school students who are sophomores or above.
Target: High school students.
Amount: $200 - $3,000
Number: Varies
Based on Financial Need: No
Deadline: June
Applications are available online from local chapters of Sons of the American Revolution.

---

(44) Kohl's Kids Who Care Scholarship
Kohls Corporation
N56 W17000 Ridgewood Drive
Menomonee Falls, WI 53051
Phone: 262-703-7000
Fax: 262-703-7115
Email: community.relations@kohls.com
URL: http://www.kohlscorporation.com/communityrelations/scholarship/index.asp
Goal: To reward young people for their contributions to their community.
Eligibility: Applicants must be nominated by a parent, educators, or community members. There is a category for kids ages 6 - 12 and another for kids ages 13-18. Applicants must not have graduated from high school.
Target: Junior high students or younger, High school students.

Amount: Up to $10,000
Number: At least 2,100
Based on Financial Need: No
Deadline: March
Applications are available at Kohl's stores and online.

---

(45) Leaders and Achievers Scholarship Program
Comcast
1500 Market Street
Philadelphia, PA 19102
Phone: 800-266-2278
URL:http://www.comcast.com
Goal: To assist graduating high school seniors who take leadership roles in their school and help improve their community with service.
Eligibility: Applicants must be high school seniors with a GPA of 2.8 or above, be nominated by their principal or guidance counselor and attend school in a Comcast community. The website has a list of eligible communities broken down by state.
Employees and family of Comcast and it's affiliates are not eligible.
Target: High school students.
Amount: $1,000
Number: Varies
Based on Financial Need: No
Deadline: Unknown
Applications are available from the principal or counselor who gave the nomination.

---

(46) Letters About Literature Contest
Letters About Literature

P.O. Box 5308
Woodbridge, VA 22194
Email: programdirector@lettersaboutliterature.org
URL:http://www.lettersaboutliterature.org
Goal: To encourage young students to read.
Eligibility: Applicants must be legal U.S. residents in grades 4 through 12 and be at least nine years old by the September 1 that precedes the award deadline. Each applicant must submit a personal letter to an author about how the author's work impacted them.
Target: Junior high and younger, High school students.
Amount: $100 to $500
Number: 18
Based on Financial Need: No
Deadline: January
Entry instructions are available online. A letter and entry coupon are required to apply.

---

(47) Love Your Body Poster Contest

National Organization for Women Foundation
LYB Poster Contest
1100 H Street, NW
Suite 300
Washington, DC 20005
URL:http://www.nowfoundation.org
Goal: To acknowledge those who create posters encouraging women to love their bodies.
Eligibility: Applicants my be students at any level or non-students from any country. Applicants must create a poster that challenges the stereotypical, limiting and negative portrayals of women in the media.

Target: Junior high and younger, High school, College, Graduate and Adult students.
Amount: Varies
Number: 4
Based on Financial Need: No
Deadline: December
Application information is available online.

---

(48) LULAC General Awards

League of United Latin American Citizens
2000 L Street NW Suite 610
Washington, DC 20036
Phone: 202-835-9646
Fax: 202-835-9685
Email: scholarships@lnesc.org
URL:http://www.lnesc.org
Goal: To assist students who are working towards a degree.
Eligibility: Applicants can be of any ethnic background. Students must be U.S. citizens or legal residents, enrolled or applied to a two or four-year college, university or graduate school. While grades and academic achievement can be considered, the main focus of the award is motivation, sincerity and integrity shown through the interview and the essay.
Target: High school, College, Graduate and Adult students.
Amount: $250 to $1,000
Number: Varies
Based on Financial Need: No
Deadline: March
Applications are available online.

(49) LULAC Honors Awards
League of United Latin American Citizens
2000 L Street NW Suite 610
Washington, DC 20036
Phone: 202-835-9646
Fax: 202-835-9685
Email: scholarships@lnesc.org
URL:http://www.lnesc.org
Goal: To assist students in all levels of higher education.
Eligibility: Applicants can be of any ethnicity. Applicants must be U.S. Citizens or legal residents, with a GPA of 3.25 or higher and have applied to or enrolled at a college, university or graduate school. Applicants who are entering freshman must have an ACT score of 23 or higher or an SAT score of 1000 or higher.
Target: High school, College, Graduate and Adult students.
Amount: $250 to $2,000
Number: Varies
Based on Financial Need: No
Deadline: March
Applications are available online.

---

(50) LULAC National Scholastic Achievement Awards
League of United Latin American Citizens
2000 L Street NW Suite 610
Washington, DC 20036
Phone: 202-835-9646
Fax: 202-835-9685
Email: scholarships@lnesc.org
URL:http://www.lnesc.org

Goal: To assist students who are attending colleges, universities or graduate schools.

Eligibility: Applicants can be of any ethnicity. Applicants must be U.S. citizens or legal residents and have applied or enrolled in any college, university or graduate school. Students must have a 3.5 GPA or higher and entering freshman must have an ACT score of 29 or higher or an SAT score of 1350 or higher. A local (state) LULAC Council in the applicants state is required to apply.

Target: College, Graduate, and Adult students.

Amount: Up to $2,000

Number: Varies

Based on Financial Need: No

Deadline: March

Applications are available online.

---

(51) Most Valuable Student Scholarships

Elks National Foundation Headquarters

2750 North Lakeview Avenue

Chicago, IL 60614

Phone: 773-755-4732

Fax: 773-755-4733

Email: scholarship@elks.org

URL:http://www.elks.org

Goal: To assist high school seniors with financial need and demonstrated scholarship and leadership.

Eligibility: Applicants must be high school seniors who are U.S. citizens and are planning to pursue a four-year degree on a full time basis at a U.S. college or university.

Target: High school students.

Amount: $1,000 to $15,000

Number: 500

Scholarship can be renewed.
Based on Financial Need: Yes
Deadline: December
To apply contact your local Elks association.

---

(52) Nancy Reagan Pathfinder Scholarships
National Federation of Republican Women
124 N. Alfred Street
Alexandria, VA 22314
Phone: 703-548-9688
Fax: 703-548-9836
Email: mail@nfrw.org
URL:http://www.nfrw.org/programs/scholarships.htm
Goal: To honor former First Lady Nancy Reagan.
Eligibility: Applicants must be college sophomores or above, including master's degree students.
Target: College, Graduate and Adult students.
Amount: $2,500
Number: 3
Based on Financial Need: No
Deadline: June
Applications are available online. A completed application, three letters of recommendation, transcript, two essays and State Federation President Certification are required.

---

(53) National College Match Program
QuestBridge
120 Hawthrone Avenue Suite 103
Palo Alto, CA 94301
Phone: 888-275-2054

Fax: 650-653-2516
Email: questions@questbridge.org
URL:http://www.questbridge.org
Goal: To help low income high school seniors with admission and full four year scholarships to top colleges.
Eligibility: Applicants must have demonstrated academic excellence and financial need. Students from all backgrounds and races are encouraged to apply.
Target: High school students.
Amount: Varies
Number: Varies
Scholarship can be renewable..
Based on Financial Need: Yes
Deadline: September
Applications are available online beginning in August. A completed application, two teacher recommendations, one counselor recommendation, a transcript and SAT and/or ACT score reports are required.

---

(54) National D-Day Museum Online Essay Contest
National D-Day Museum Foundation
945 Magazine Street
New Orleans, LA 70130
Phone: 504-527-6012
Fax: 504-527-6088
Email: info@nationalww2museum.org
URL:http://www.ddaymuseum.org
Goal: To increase knowledge of World War II by giving students the chance to compete in an essay contest.

Eligibility: Applicants must be high school students and write an essay of 1,000 or less on a topic selected by the sponsor. Only the first 500 essays will be accepted.
Target: High school students.
Amount: $250 - $1,000
Number: 6
Based on Financial Need: No
Deadline: March
Applications are available online.

---

(55) National History Day Contest
National History Day
University of Maryland
4511 Knox Road
Suite 205
College Park, MD 20740
Phone: 301-314-9739
Fax: 301-314-9767
Email: info@nhd.org
URL:http://www.nationalhistoryday.org
Goal: To acknowledge students for their scholarship, initiative and cooperation.
Eligibility: Applicants must be in grades 6-12 and prepare history presentations throughout the year that are based on an annual theme. In February or March students compete in a district History Day contest. The winners then compete in a state contest usually in April or May. Those winners compete at the national level in June at the University of Maryland.
Target: Junior high and younger and High school students.
Amount: Varies
Number: Varies

Based on Financial Need: No
Deadline: Unknown
Applications are available online.

---

(56) National Merit Scholarship Program and National Achievement Scholarship Program

National Merit Scholarship Corporation
1560 Sherman Avenue Suite 200
Evanston, IL 60201
Phone: 847-866-5100
Fax: 847-866-5113
URL:http://www.nationalmerit.org
Goal: To assist student with educational expenses through a merit based competition.
Eligibility: Applicants must be in high school and on the typical track towards completion and planning to enter college by the fall following graduation from high school. Applicants must be U.S. citizens, legal residents or in the process of becoming a U.S. citizen. Participation in the scholarship is based on the PSAT/NMSQT exam which must be taken by the 11th grade.
Target: High school students.
Amount: $2,500
Number: Varies
Scholarship can be renewed.
Based on Financial Need: No
Deadline: October, PSAT test date.
Application is made by taking the PSAT.

---

(57) Odenza Marketing Scholarship

Odenza Vacations

4664 Lougheed Highway Suite 230
Burnaby, BC V5C 5T5
Phone: 877-297-2661
URL: http://www.odenzascholarships.com
Goal: To assist college students and future college students between the ages of 16 and 25 with their college expenses.
Eligibility: Applicants must be U.S. or Canadian citizens with at least one year of college remaining. Applicants must have a GPA of 2.5 or higher.
Target: High school, College and Graduate students.
Amount: $500
Number: Varies
Based on Financial Need: No
Deadline: March
Applications are available online. A completed application and two essays are required to apply.

---

(58) Off to College Scholarship Sweepstakes
Sun Trust
P.O. Box 27172
Richmond, VA 23261
Phone: 800-786-8787
URL: http://www.suntrusteducation.com
Goal: To assist students with their first year college expenses.
Eligibility: Applicants must be high school seniors (at least 13 years old) who are planning to attending a college or university accredited by the U.S. Department of Education in the fall following their graduation. Winners are chosen at random every two weeks.
Target: High school students.
Amount: $1,000

Number: 15
Based on Financial Need: No
Deadline: May
Applications are available online.

---

(59) OP Loftbed Scholarship Award
OP Loftbed
P.O. Box 573
Thomasville, NC 27361
Phone: 866-567-5638
Email: info@oploftbed.com
URL:http://www.oploftbed.com
Goal: To acknowledge students who show excellence in creative writing.
Eligibility: Applicants must be U.S. citizens who plan to attend an accredited college or university in the upcoming school year.
Target: High school, College and Adult students.
Amount: $500
Number: Varies
Based on Financial Need: No
Deadline: July
Applications are available online. A completed application and essay are required to apply.

---

(60) Optimist International Contest
Optimist International
4494 Lindell Boulevard
St. Louis, MO 63108
Phone: 314-371-6000
Fax: 314-371-6006
Email: programs@optimist.org

URL:http://www.optimist.org
Goal: To assist students for their writing skills.
Eligibility: Applicants must be under 18 on December 31 of the current school year. Applicants must write an essay on a sponsor specified topic and apply through a local Optimist Club. Students will compete at the local, district and international level.
Target: High school students.
Amount: $2,500
Number: Varies
Based on Financial Need: No
Deadline: February
Contact your local Optimist Club.

---

(61) Optimist International Oratorical Contest
Optimist International
4494 Lindell Boulevard
St. Louis, MO 63108
Phone: 314-371-6000
Fax: 314-371-6006
Email: program@optimist.org
URL:http://www.optimist.org
Goal: To assist students based on their oratorical skills.
Eligibility: Applicants must be students in the U.S. Canada or Caribbean who are under 16 years old on the last day of the year.
Target: Junior high and younger and High school students.
Amount: $1,000 - $2,500
Number: 3
Based on Financial Need: No
Deadline: March and June

Contact your local Optimist Club.

---

(62) Parent Answer Scholarship Sweepstakes
Parent Answer Scholarship Sweepstakes
P.O. Box 9500
Wilkes-Barre, PA 18773
URL:http://www.collegeanswer.com
Goal: To assist the parents of college students.
Eligibility: Applicants must be U.S. residents and parents of undergraduate college students at a Title IV school. Applicants must sign up for the Sallie Mae Parent Answer e-Newsletter.
Target: College and Adult students.
Amount: $10,000
Number: 1
Based on Financial Need: No
Deadline: May
Applicants may enter the sweepstakes online or by mail.

---

(63) Patriot's Pen Youth Essay Contest
Veterans of Foreign Wars
406 W. 34th Street
Kansas City, MO 64111
Phone: 816-968-1117
Fax: 816-968-1149
Email: kharmer@vfw.org
URL:http://www.vfw.org
Goal: To assist students grades 6 to 8.

Eligibility: Applicants must be in 6th - 8th grade in a public, home schooled or private school in the U.S. or its territories. To apply applicants must write an essay based on a topic that is determined by the sponsor.
Target: Junior high and younger.
Amount: Up to $10,000
Number: Varies
Based on Financial Need: No
Deadline: November
Applications are available online or at your local VFW post.

---

(64) Phoenix Scholarship Program
Phoenix Scholarship Program
159 Concord Avenue Suite IC
Cambridge, MA 02138
Email: phoenixawards@gmail.com
Goal: To assist deserving high school seniors planning to pursue higher education.
Eligibility: Applicants must be U.S. high school seniors or high school graduates who have graduated within 13 months of the application deadline. Applicants must have a GPA of 2.75 or higher and have taken the SAT or ACT. Applicants must be in good standing at their high school and show good morals and enroll in an accredited college or university after high school graduation.
Target: High school students
Amount: Varies
Number: Up to 4
Based on Financial Need: No
Deadline: April
Applications are available via email.

(65) Platt Family Scholarship Prize Essay Contest

The Lincoln Forum
c/o Don McCue, Curator of the Lincoln Memorial Shrine
125 West Vine Street
Redlands, CA 92373
Phone: 909-798-7632
Email: archives@akspl.org
URL:http://www.thelincolnforum.org
Goal: To assist students who have written the best essay on Abraham Lincoln.
Eligibility: Applicants must be full-time undergraduate students enrolled in a U.S. college or university in the spring term and they must submit an essay on a sponsor determined topic.
Target: College and Adult students.
Amount: $500 - $1,500
Number: 3
Based on Financial Need: No
Deadline: July
Applications are available online. A completed application and essay are required to apply.

(66) Poster Contest for High School Students

Christophers
12 E. 48th Street
New York, NY 10017
URL:http://www.christophers.org
Goal: To acknowledge students for exploring a theme in poster art.

Eligibility: Applicants must be high school students and they must submit a poster of original content that explores the sponsors theme.
Target: High school students
Amount: $500 - $1,000
Number: Up to 8
Based on Financial Need: No
Deadline: February
Applications are available online.

---

(67) Principal's Leadership Award

Herff Jones
c/o National Association of Secondary School Principals
1904 Association Drive
Reston, VA 20191
Phone: 800-253-7746
Email: carrollw@principals.org
URL:http://www.principals.org/awards/
Goal: To acknowledge students for their leadership.
Eligibility: Applicants must be high school seniors who have been nominated by their high school principal. Each principal can nominate one student from their high school.
Target: High school students.
Amount: $1,000 to $12,000
Number: 100
Based on Financial Need: No
Deadline: December
Nomination forms are available online.

---

(68) Prize in Ethics Essay Contest

Elie Wiesel Foundation for Humanity
55 Madison Avenue
New York NY 10022
Phone: 212-490-7788
Fax: 212-490-7788
Email: info@eliewieselfoundation.org
URL:http://www.eliewieselfoundation.org
Goal: To encourage the though and discussion of ethics and their role in education.
Eligibility: Applicants must be full time juniors or seniors at a U.S. accredited college or university and are required to write an essay on ethics. A faculty sponsor is required to review and sign the student's entry form.
Target: College and Adult students.
Amount: $2,500 - $5,000
Number: 5
Based on Financial Need: No
Deadline: December
Applications are available online.

---

(69) Project on Nuclear Issues Essay Contest
Center for Strategic and International Studies
Project on Nuclear Issues
1800 K Street, NW
Washington, DC 20006
Phone: 202-887-0200
Fax: 202-775-3199
Email: jward@csis.org
URL:http://www.csis.org
Goal: To assist those who have written the best essay on nuclear weapons.

Eligibility: Applicants must be undergraduate, graduate or recent college graduate and submit an essay covering some aspect of nuclear weapons or strategy.
Target: College, Graduate and Adult students.
Amount: $1,500 - $5,000
Number: 4
Based on Financial Need: No
Deadline: Varies
Applications are available online.

---

(70) Project Vote Smart National Internship Program
Project Vote Smart
Internship Coordinator
1 Common Ground
Philipsburg, MT 59858
Phone: 406-859-8683
Fax: 406-859-8680
Email: intern@votesmart.org
URL:http://www.votesmart.org
Goal: To encourage college students and recent graduates to develop an interest in voter education.
Eligibility: Applicants must be current college students or recent college graduates who are able to willing to use a non-partisan attitude when doing voter education in a ten-week internship.
Target: College and Adult students.
Amount: All Living Costs
Number: Varies
Based on Financial Need: No
Deadline: Rolling

Applications are available online. A completed application, resume, essay and three references are required to apply.

---

(71) Proof-Reading.com Scholarship
Proof-Reading Inc.
12 Geary Street Suite 806
San Francisco, CA 94108
Phone: 866-433-4867
Email: support@proof-reading.com
URL:http://www.proof-reading.com
Goal: To acknowledge outstanding student essayists.
Eligibility: Applicants must be U.S. legal residents who are full time students at an accredited college or university with a 3.5 GPA or higher. Applicants must submit an essay on a topic determined by the sponsor.
Target: College and Adult students.
Amount: $1,500
Number: 1
Based on Financial Need: No
Deadline: June
Applications are available online. A completed application and essay are required.

---

(72) Prudential Spirit of Community Awards
Prudential Spirit of Community Awards
Prudential Financial Inc.
751 Broad Street, 16th Floor
Newark, NJ 07102
Phone: 877-525-8491
Email: spirit@prudential.com
URL:http://spirit.comprudential.com

Goal: To acknowledge students for their volunteer work in their community.
Eligibility: Applicants must be students grades 5-12 and a legal U.S. resident participating in volunteer work that in part occurred in the year before the date of application.
Target: Junior high and younger and High school students.
Amount: $1,000 to $5,000
Number: 102
Based on Financial Need: No
Deadline: November
Applications are available online.

---

(73) Religious Liberty Essay Scholarship Contest
Baptist Joint Committee for Religious Liberty
Essay Contest
200 Maryland Avenue NE
Washington, DC 20002
Phone: 202-544-4226
Fax: 202-544-2094
Email: ccrowe@bjconline.org
URL:http://www.bjconline.org
Goal: To acknowledge students who have written outstanding essays about religious liberty.
Eligibility: Applicants must be high school juniors or seniors and must submit a 800 to 1,200 word essay on a topic that is related to religious freedom.
Target: High school students.
Amount: $100 to $1,000
Number: 3
Based on Financial Need: No
Deadline: March

Applications are available online. A registration form and essay are required to apply.

---

(74) Return 2 College Scholarship
R2C Scholarship Program
URL:http://www.return2college.com/awardprogram.cfm
Goal: To assist college and adult students with educational expenses.
Eligibility: Applicants must be college or adult students who are attending or planning to attend a two or four-year college or graduate school in the next 12 months. Applicants must be at least 17 years old and U.S citizens or permanent residents.
Target: High school, College and Adult students.
Amount: $1,500
Number: Varies
Based on Financial Need: No
Deadline: March, August, December
Applications are available online.

---

(75) Ronald McDonald House Charities U.S. Scholarships
Ronald McDonald House Charities
1321 Murfreesboro Road Suite 800
Nashville, TN 37217
Phone: 855-670-ISTS
Email: contactus@applyists.com
URL:http://www.rmhc.org
Goal: To assist high school seniors with educational expenses.

Eligibility: Applicants must be high school seniors younger than 21 years oldwith a GPA of 2.7 or higher. Applicants must reside in a Ronald McDonald House Charities chapter area. Four scholarships are available RMHC/Scholars, RMHC/Asia, RMHC/African-American Future Achievers and RMHC/HACER.
Target: High school students.
Amount: $1,000
Number: Varies
Based on Financial Need: Yes
Deadline: December
Applications are available online. A completed application, transcripts, parents tax forms, letter of recommendation and personal statement are required to apply.

---

(76) Ruth Stanton Community Grant
Action Volunteering
Ruth Stanton Community Grant
P.O. Box 1013
Calimesa, CA 92320
Email: painter5@ipsemail.com
URL:http://www.actionvolunteering.com
Goal: To assist students in performing community service activities.
Eligibility: Applicants must be active in performing community service work.
Target: High school, College, Graduate and Adult students.
Amount: $500
Number: Varies
Based on Financial Need: No
Deadline: May

Applications are available online. A completed application, essay and letter of recommendation are required to apply.

---

(77) Sally Strain Memorial Scholarship

The Online Degree Advisor
P.O. Box 2790
Turlock, CA 95380
Email: scholarship@theonlinedegreeadvisor.com
URL:http://www.theonlinedegreeadvisor.com
Goal: To assist students with their educational expenses.
Eligibility: Applicants must be 17 years old or older and planning to attend school in the next 12 months. Students can be majoring in any field and can be attending online or in person.
Target: High school, College, Graduate and Adult students.
Amount: $100
Number: 1
Based on Financial Need: No
Deadline: August
Applications are available online.

---

(78) Samuel Huntington Public Service Award

National Grid
25 Research Drive
Westborough, MA 01582
Phone: 508-389-2000
URL:http://www.nationalgridus.com
Goal: To assist students who are willing to perform one year of humanitarian service after graduation.

Eligibility: Applicants must be graduating college seniors and willing to perform one year of humanitarian service in the U.S. or abroad. The service can be through a charity, religious group, education or government organization.
Target: College and Adult students.
Amount: $10,000
Number: Varies
Based on Financial Need: No
Deadline: January
Applications are available online.

---

(79) SanDisk Foundation Scholarship Program
SanDisk Foundation Scholarship Program
c/o International Scholarship and Tuition Service Inc
1321 Murfreesboro Road Suite 800
Nashville, TN 37217
Phone: 855-670-ISTS
Email: contactus@applyists.com
URL:http://www.sandisk.com/about-sandisk/corporate-social-responsibility/community-engagement/sandisk-scholars-fund
Goal: To assist students with demonstrated leadership and entrepreneurial interests.
Eligibility: Applicants must be high school seniors or college junior or below and must attend or be planning to attend a full-time undergraduate degree program with demonstrated financial need. As many as 27 $2,500 renewable scholarships are available to the public. As many as 3 $2,500 scholarships are available for dependents of SanDisk employees and two applicants will be chosen as "SanDisk Scholars" and will be awarded full tuition scholarships for up to four years.

Target: High school, College and Adult students.
Amount: $2,500 to Full tuition.
Number: Up to 30
Scholarship can be renewed.
Based on Financial Need: Yes
Deadline: March
Applications are available online. A completed application and essay are required to apply.

(80) Scholarship Drawing for $1,000
Edsouth
eCampusTours
P.O. Box 36014
Knoxville, TN 37930
Phone: 865-342-0670
Fax:
Email: info@ecampustours.com
URL:http://www.ecampustours.com
Goal: To help students pay for college.
Eligibility: Applicants must be U.S. citizens or legal residents enrolled in a higher education institution. The winner must be enrolled in an eligible institution within one year of the award.
Target: High school, College, Graduate and Adult students.
Amount: $1,000
Number: 2
Based on Financial Need: No
Deadline: March
Applications are available online.

(81) Scholarship Slam
Power Poetry

295 E. 8th Street Suite 3W
New York, NY 10009
Phone:
Fax:
Email: help@powerpoetry.org
URL:http://powerpoetry.org/poetry-slams/scholarship
Goal: To acknowledge students who write a slam poem.
Eligibility: Applicants must be 25 years old or younger and U.S. citizens.
Target: High school, College and Graduate students.
Amount: $1,000
Number: 1
Based on Financial Need: No
Deadline: November
Applicants must join the website and submit their poem.

---

(82) Second Chance Scholarship Contest
American Fire Sprinkler Association
12750 Merit Drive
Suite 350
Dallas, TX 75251
Phone: 214-349-5965
Fax: 214-343-8898
Email: acampbell@firesprinkler.org
URL:http://www.afsascholarship.org
Goal: To assist students in paying for educational costs.

Eligibility: Applicants must be U.S citizens or legal residents, high school graduates or GED recipients who are enrolled at a college or university by the spring of the upcoming academic year. The award is determined by random drawing.

Target: College, Graduate and Adult students.

Amount: $1,000

Number: 5

Based on Financial Need: No

Deadline: August

Applicants must read an article on fire sprinklers and take a ten question test. The number of correct responses is the number of entries that are made.

---

(83) Shut Up and Sweat Athletic Gear Student Athlete Annual Scholarship

No Excuses Wear

c/o Student Athlete Scholarship Committee

976 Lake Isabella Way

San Jose, CA 95123

Phone: 408-927-7027

Email: noexcuseswear@yahoo.com

URL:http://www.noexcuseswear.com

Goal: To assist college bound high school students.

Eligibility: Applicants must be high school seniors who are athletes with a GPA of 3.0 or higher.

Target: High school students.

Amount: Varies

Number: Varies

Based on Financial Need: No

Deadline: August

Application instructions are available online. A nomination letter, transcripts and a list of extracurricular activities are required.

(84) Signet Classic Student Scholarship Essay Contest
Penguin Group
Academic Marketing Department
375 Hudson Street
New York, NY 10014
URL: http://us.penguingroup.com/static/html/services -academic/essayhome.html
Goal: To acknowledge high school students for their essays on literature.
Eligibility: Applicants must be high school juniors or seniors and submit an essay on one of five topics that are selected by the sponsor regarding a piece of literature. Each English teacher may submit one junior and one senior essay.
Target: High school students.
Amount: $1,000
Number: 5
Based on Financial Need: No
Deadline: April
English teachers or the parent of a home schooled student may submit essays.

(85) SOAR Scholarship
Students Overcoming Adversity Responsibly
P.O. Box 481030
Charlotte, NC 28269
Email: emergedevelopment2@yahoo.com

URL:http://www.adriannemccauley.com/scholarship.
html
Goal: To assist students who have overcome
adversity.
Eligibility: Applicants must be U.S. citizens who are
high school seniors who will graduate in the year of
their application.
Target: High school students.
Amount: $1,000
Number: 1
Based on Financial Need: No
Deadline: April
Applications are available online. An completed
application and essay are required to apply.

---

(86) Standout Student College Scholarship
College Peas LLC
1210 Forest Avenue
Highland Park, IL 60035
Phone: 847-681-0698
URL:http://www.collegepeas.com
Goal: To assist college bound high school students
whose interests make them stand out from their peers.
Eligibility: Appicants must be current high school
students with a GPA of 2.0 or higher and plan to
enroll in a four year college or university full time.
Target: High school students.
Amount: $500
Number: Varies
Based on Financial Need: No
Deadline: January
Applications are available online. A completed
application and essay are required to apply.

(87) Stephen J. Brady STOP Hunger Scholarship
Sodexo Foundation
9801 Washingtonian Boulevard
Gaithersburg, MD 20878
Phone: 800-763-3946
Email: stophunger@sodexofoundation.org
URL:http://www.sodexofoundation.org
Goal: To assist students who have been active in the movement to end hunger.
Eligibility: Applicants must be U.S. citizens or permanent residents who are in kindergarten to graduate school enrolled at an accredited U.S. institution. Applicants must have been active in at least one unpaid volunteer effort to end hunger within the past 12 months. Previous recipients and Sodexo employees are not eligible for the award.
Target: Junior high students or younger, High school, College, Graduate and Adult students.
Amount: $5,000
Number: Varies
Based on Financial Need: No
Deadline: December
Applications are available online. A completed application and supporting documents are required to apply.

(88) Stokes Educational Scholarship Program
National Security Agency
9800 Savage Road, Suite 6779
Ft. George G. Meade, MD 20755
Phone: 410-854-4725

URL:http://www.nsa.gov
Goal: To recruit individuals, especially minority high school seniors, with skills that are useful to the NSA.
Eligibility: Applicants must be high school seniors at the time of the application, be U.S. citizens, have a GPA of 3.0 or higher, with a minimum ACT score or 25 or SAT score of 1600. Applicants must have demonstrated leadership skills and planning to major in computer science or computer electrical engineering.
Target: High school students.
Amount: Full tuition, fees, salary and summer employment.
Number: Varies
Scholarship can be renewed.
Based on Financial Need: No
Deadline: November
Applications are available online.

---

(89) Stuck at Prom Scholarship
Henkel Consumer Adhesives
32150 Just Imagine Drive
Avon, OH 44011
URL:http://www.stuckatprom.com
Goal: To acknowledge students for their creative use of duct tape.
Eligibility: Applicants must attend high school prom as a couple wearing attire made of duct tape. The award is given to the most original attire.
Target: High school students.
Amount: $500 - $3,000
Number: Varies
Based on Financial Need: No
Deadline: June

Applications are available online. A prom picture and contact information are required to apply.

---

(90) SuperCollege Scholarship
SuperCollege.com
2713 Newlands Avenue
Belmont, CA 94002
Email: supercollege@supercollege.com
URL:http://www.supercollege.com/scholarship
Goal: To assist high school, college and graduate students with their educational expenses.
Eligibility: Applicants must be high school, college or graduate students in the U.S. who are planning or attending a college or university within the next 12 months. The scholarship can be used of tuition, books, room and board, computers or other educational expenses.
Target: High school, College, Graduate and Adult students.
Amount: $1,500
Number: 1
Based on Financial Need: No
Deadline: March, July, October, December
Applications are available online.

---

(91) The Lowe's Scholarship
Lowe's Company
1000 Lowe's Boulevard
Mooreseville, NC 28117
Phone: 800-44-LOWES
URL:http://www.careers.lowes.com/college_recruiting_scholarship.aspx

Goal: To assist high school students in communities where Lowe's operates stores to pay for educational expenses.

Eligibility: Applicants must be high school seniors planning to enroll in an accredited two or four year college or university in the U.S. Selection of the award is based on leadership abilities, community involvement and academic achievement.

Target: High school students.

Amount: $2,500

Number: 140

Scholarship can be renewed.

Based on Financial Need: No

Deadline: February

Applications are available online.

---

(92) TruFit Good Citizenship Scholarship

Citizens Bank

URL:http://www.citizensbank.com/scholarship/

Goal: To assist high school seniors and college students who have volunteered their time.

Eligibility: Applicants must be at least 16 years old and attended or have been accepted into a nationally accredited four year college, university or graduate program.

Target: High school, College, Graduate and Adult students.

Amount: $1,000 - $5,000

Number: 40

Based on Financial Need: No

Deadline: April

Applications are available online. An essay or video are required to apply.

(93) U.S. Bank Scholarship Program
U.S. Bank
U.S. Bancorp Center
800 Nicollet Mall
Minneapolis, MN 55402
Phone: 800-242-1200
URL:http://www.usbank.com/student-lending/scholarship.html
Goal: To assist high school seniors who plan to attend college.
Eligibility: Applicants must be high school seniors who are planning to attend a college or university or current college freshman, sophomores or juniors who are currently attending full-time an accredited two year or four year college or university and be U.S. citizens or permanent residents. The award is determined by a random drawing.
Target: High school, College and Adult students.
Amount: $1,000
Number: 40
Based on Financial Need: No
Deadline: March
Applications are available online.

---

(94) U.S JCI Senate Scholarship Grants
U.S. JCI Senate
106 Wedgewood Drive
Carrollton, GA 30117
Email: tom@smipc.net
URL:http://www.usjcisenate.org

Goal: To assist high school students who want to continue their education.

Eligibility: Applicants must be high school seniors who are planning to attend college full time, U.S. citizens and graduating from a U.S. high school, approved home school or GED test.

Target: High school students.

Amount: $1,000

Number: Varies

Based on Financial Need: No

Deadline: December -January

Applications are available from the guidance office.

---

(95) Undergraduate Transfer Scholarship

Jack Kent Cooke Foundation Undergraduate Transfer Scholarship

44325 Woodridge Parkway

Lansdowne, VA 20176

Phone: 800-498-6478

Fax: 319-337-1204

Email: jkc-u@act.org

URL:http://www.jkcf.org

Goal: To assist community college students so that they may attend a four-year university.

Eligibility: Applicants must be students or recent alumni from an accredited U.S. community or junior college who are planning to pursue a bachelors degree at a four year college or university. Applicants must be nominated by the Jack Kent Cooke Foundation faculty rep at their school. Applicants must have a GPA of 3.5 or higher.

Target: College or Adult students.

Amount: Up to $30,000

Number: 50

Scholarship can be renewed.
Based on Financial Need: No
Deadline: December
Applications are available online and mailed in.

---

(96) University Language Services College Scholarship
University Language Services
15 Maiden Lane Suite 300
New York, NY 10038
Phone: 800-419-4601
Fax: 866-662-8048
Email: service@universitylanguage.com
URL:http://www.universitylanguage.com
Goal: To assist college bound high school students.
Eligibility: Applicants must be high school students at an accredited high school. Applicants must submit a photo that they have taken while visiting a college campus along with a description of how the photo shows college life.
Target: High school students.
Amount: $100- $500
Number: 3
Based on Financial Need: No
Deadline: October
Applications information is available online.

---

(97) Visine Students with Vision Scholarship Program
Johnson and Johnson Healthcare Products
c/o International Scholarship and Tuition Service Inc
1321 Murfreesboro Road Suite 800

Nashville, TN 37217
Phone: 855-670-ISTS
Email: contactus@applyists.com
URL:http://www.visine.com/scholarship
Goal: To assist students who have a vision that is effectively communicated through essay or video.
Eligibility: Applicants must be high school seniors or college freshman, sophomore or juniors and show involvement in school and community. Students must show financial need and be able to demonstrate their vision through an essay or video. A GPA of 2.8 or above is required.
Target: High school, College and Adult students.
Amount: $5,000
Number: Up to 10
Based on Financial Need: No
Deadline: March
Applications are available online.

---

(98) Wendy's High School Helsman Award
Wendy's Restaurants
Phone: 800-205-6367
Email: wendys@act.org
URL:http://www.wendyshighschoolheisman.com
Goal: To acknowledge high school students who have excelled in academics, athletics and student leadership.
Eligibility: Applicants must be beginning their high school senior year and have participated in one of the 27 sanctioned sports. Students must have a GPA of 3.0 or higher. Award selection is based on academics, community service and athletic accomplishments.
Target: High school students.
Amount: Varies

Number: Varies
Based on Financial Need: No
Deadline: October
Applications are available online.

---

(99) Where's FRANKIE the Diploma Frame? Scholarship Photo Contest

Church Hill Classics
594 Pepper Street
Monroe, CT 06468
Phone: 800-447-9005
Fax: 203-268-2468
Email: info@diplomaframe.com
URL:http://www.framemyfuture.com
Goal: To assist college students with the costs of textbooks.
Eligibility: Applicants must be legal U.S. residents who are 18 years old or above and full-time college students or the family member of full-time college students. Applicants must submit a photo showing the sponsor's mascot participating in a summer activity. Award selection is based on the creativity and popularity of the photo.
Target: College, Graduate and Adult students.
Amount: $500 Gift Card
Number: 3
Based on Financial Need: No
Deadline: August
Applications are available online.

---

(100) William E. Simon Fellowship for Noble Purpose

Intercollegiate Studies Institute
3901 Centerville Road
Wilmington, DE 19807
Phone: 800-526-7022
Fax: 302-652-1760
Email: simon@isi.org
URL:http://www.isi.org
Goal: To assist graduating college seniors who are committed to strengthening civil society.
Eligibility: Applicants must be graduating college seniors with self directed plans to improve society. Award selection is based on academics, recommendations, extracurricular activities and project goals.
Target: College and Adult students.
Amount: $40,000
Number: 1
Based on Financial Need: No
Deadline: January
Applications are available online. A completed application, essay, transcript, recommendation letters, and outline of educational achievements are required.

---

(101) Win Free Tuition Giveaway
Next Step Magazine
86 W. Main Street
Victor, NY 14565
Phone: 800-771-3117
Email: webcopy@nextstepmag.com
URL:http://www.nextstepmagazine.com/winfreetuition
Goal: To support higher education.

Eligibility: Applicants must be legal U.S. or Canadian residents who are 14 or older who are planning to enroll in college by September 30th, 3 years after the application date. The award is an annual sweepstakes for one year's tuition up to $10,000 and 11 monthly $1,000 drawings.
Target: High school, College, Graduate and Adult students.
Amount: $1,000 - $10,000
Number: 12
Based on Financial Need: No
Deadline: June
Applications are available online.